D1579829

Dedication

To my first grandson, Rafe Sabian Bennett, whose gestation coincided with that of this book. Born in England, like his father, David, and uncle, John, but qualified, should he have the desire and ability, to become a Welsh Rugby Hero.

Welsh

It's Wales

Rugby
Heroes

Androw Bennett

y Lolfa

Thanks to:

The Western Mail, S4C and the National Library of Wales

for the photographs

First impression: 2002
Second impression: 2003
© Copyright Androw Bennett and Y Lolfa Cyf.,2002

Cover design: Ceri Jones

This book is subject to copyright and may not be reproduced by any method, except for review purposes, without the prior, written consent of the publishers.

ISBN: 0 86243 552 8

Printed on acid free and partly recycled paper
and published and bound in Wales by:
Y Lolfa Cyf., Talybont, Ceredigion SY24 5AP
e-mail ylolfa@ylolfa.com
internet www.ylolfa.com
phone +44 (0)1970 832 304
fax 832 782
isdn 832 813

Contents

Introduction   7

15: Full Back   9

Wings   13

Centres   19

10: Outside-Half   27

9: Scrum-Half   33

No. 8   39

Flanker   45

Second Row   51

Hooker   57

Prop Forwards   62

Post Script   68

Carwyn James

Introduction

S ome will argue that Welsh rugby heroes are a long-forgotten species, their aspiring successors also-rans in a professional era which has seen the Celtic nations little more than bit-part players on the world rugby scene. Trailing in the wake of the great Southern Hemisphere teams – New Zealand, Australia and South Africa – and France and England, Welsh rugby has been in the doldrums, some will argue, for far too long.

The memories of heroes departed from the pitch, some in the now distant past, may inspire future generations of players to greater effort and thus greater success. This book looks back at the heroes of the second half of the 20th century for just such inspiration.

It will doubtless give rise to more arguments as to who was 'The Greatest' and while reference may be made to such an accolade, it is not the author's intention to step into fans' firing line with his own propositions. Nor do I intend to establish a 'Greatest Team', although the reader may, from time to time, detect a note of bias in comparing players of the same or a similar generation.

It is almost impossible to compare players of different eras. The game has changed enormously over the years, particularly in the 1990s. The advent of the professional era, embraced in different ways by the rugby-playing nations of the world, tells only a part of the story.

The role of players on the field has changed too. Barry John, memorably, described the five tight forwards, playing in the front-row and second-row of the scrum, as 'donkeys' whose sole function was to maul, ruck and, indeed, fight for the ball at any and every breakdown in the flow of the game. Ball-winning and recycling possession is still the primary function of such players but you would no longer be able to throw a proverbial 'blanket' over these five 'drones' as they trundle from scrum to maul to lineout to ruck. These days, they are strung out across the width of the field, looking for opportunities to commit two or three opponents in order to release their own backs. They even hope to find themselves occasionally out on the wing, where they can demonstrate their blistering pace and leave a scattering of flailing opponents to admire their try-scoring prowess.

Other role-changes mean that it is invidious to compare players of different eras. Invariably, players fortunate enough to be part of a successful team will be thought of as having achieved more than those who did not drink as often from the cup of victory. Players such as Ieuan Evans, Robert Jones and Scott Quinnell might have been seen in an entirely different light if they had been part of a winning side.

Whatever happens to Welsh rugby in the future, the heroes of the past will remain in the memory and, while it may be too soon to talk of them in the same breath as the Princes Llywelyn, Owain Glyndŵr, Lloyd George and Gwynfor Evans or Dylan Thomas, Tom Jones and his ilk, as long as the game of rugby union is played in Wales, the names in the following pages will be held in high esteem by their fellow-countrymen.

Andrew Bennett

February 2002

J P R. Just three capital letters suffice to identify the Welsh rugby hero who, more than any other player, changed his position's role on the rugby field. Others before John Peter Rhys Williams had occasionally infiltrated the threequarter line to telling effect but nobody had done so consistently with such an injection of pace and power.

The so-called 'Australian Dispensation', prohibiting kicking the ball out of play on the full other than from behind a player's own 25-yard line, played a major part in Williams's rapid rise to stardom. Punting the ball from the hand or place-kicking were never a forte of his, so other aspects of his game just had to be better.

J P R 's readiness to turn defence into all-out attack was a new departure although Keith Jarrett's spectacular try against England at Cardiff Arms Park in April 1967 had shown what could be done if the circumstances were right. Jarrett was running at full tilt when he took the ball from an England kick and, while he could have broken his stride and kicked, it was easier for a skilful runner, who was later to play at centre for his country, to continue running. Jarrett's game-breaking try remains one of the truly great individual scores but injury and an early defection to Rugby League deprived Wales of this gifted all-round sportsman.

J P R was also, of course, a gifted all-rounder who, having won the Junior Wimbledon tennis championships, could easily have made that sport his career. Medicine beckoned, however, and he stayed to grace the game of Rugby Union throughout the 1970s. J P R broke English rugby hearts more than once. Returning to international action for Wales at Twickenham in January 1972 following his series-winning drop-goal for the Lions against the All Blacks in Auckland the previous summer, his two tries killed off the English challenge. But for the cancellation of the match against Ireland, 1972 would

J P R Williams

almost certainly have been a Grand Slam year for Wales. As it was, J P R played in three Grand Slam teams (1971, 1976 and 1978) and in six Triple Crown teams (1969, 1971 and 1976-9). He was one of several heroic Welsh full-backs of the second half of the 20th century and, in august company, can be singled out as an exceptionally successful talent.

What transformed J P R into a modern-day folk-hero was his determination to continue playing rugby, at whatever level he could, for almost twenty years after the end of his international career. This is usually the preserve of the gnarled old prop-forward who never succeeded in rising above the subs' bench of a junior club's Second XV but who carries on playing into OAP status, dreaming of trotting out behind the club captain for a league-winning crunch match against the club down the valley. To see a former Wales and British Lions star of the calibre and status of J P R doing so was nothing short of sensational. He could have rested on his laurels for the rest of his life. His love of the game and the sheer enjoyment of the physicality of the sport of Rugby Union has, however, meant that successive generations of players have been privileged to be able to say, "I played with/against J P R Williams." This has made him a totally different rugby hero to the majority.

My childhood memories are of adults extolling the virtues of Lewis Jones as the 'saviour' of Welsh rugby but he 'went North' to Rugby League to seek fame and fortune. As Jones made his way North, a young man from Bynea on the Llanelli bank of the River Loughor, Terry Davies, was preparing to assume the mantle of greatness as Wales's last line of defence. It is doubtful whether a harder (but always fair) tackler has ever played for Wales. And to think that his 'home' club, Llanelli, nearly lost him to arch-rivals, Swansea, because he could not see himself displacing the incumbent at Stradey Park, Gerwyn Williams, who was Wales's full-back at the time.

While Llanelli produced other noteworthy full-backs such as Kelvin Coslett and Terry Price, both of whom trekked northwards to play the 13-a-side game, Neath RFC produced three of the best exponents of the kicking arts associated with the position. The fair-haired Viv Evans appeared briefly on the scene in 1954 to kick Wales to some success in a short sequence of games. Graham Hodgson in the 1960s and Paul Thorburn in the 1980s were both very skilled all-round rugby players and adept goal-kickers. Neath supporters will sing the praises of these two match winners for generations to come. Hodgson's ability to judge the direction and force of the wind around a rugby ground often gained surprising territory for the 'Welsh All Blacks' while Thorburn's place kicking bore the hallmark of the mule. Supporters will always remember his extraordinary penalty kick from inside his own half at Cardiff Arms Park against Scotland. His last-minute successful conversion kick in the dying minutes of the Third-Place play-off match to give Wales victory over Australia in the inaugural World Cup, will stay in the record books as a high-water mark in Welsh rugby.

Although J P R, Lewis Jones, Price, Jarrett, Hodgson, Thorburn and other Welsh full-backs, such as Paul Wheeler (Aberavon), Roger Blyth and Mark Wyatt (both of Swansea) performed heroic deeds on numerous occasions, one Welsh full-back, Haydn Mainwaring, will always be remembered for a brief 'moment of madness' while wearing the hooped shirt of the Barbarians. In 1971 he infamously shook the Cardiff Arms Park to its foundations when tackling the Springbok, Avril Malan – helping the Baa-Baas to inflict the only defeat on the tourists 6-0.

But many would argue that the most famous tackle by a full back was by J P R on the burly French wing J P Gourdon in 1976. Having mistimed a tackle on Gourdon early in the game J P R was not to make the same mistake twice. A bone-crunching shoulder charge on Gourdon by the Welsh full-back secured a 19-13 victory for Wales. The crowd's sharp intake of breath, sympathetic to the prostrate Gallic star, was full testament to the power J P R brought to the full-back position.

Time was when rugby union wings were primarily seen as out-and-out try-scoring finishers. The simple object of the game was for forwards to win the ball and for it then to be transferred through the half-backs and centres as speedily as possible to a swift flier out near the touchline.

As T P ('Pope') Williams, the coach at one of Wales's best rugby nurseries, Llandovery College, put it succinctly to his young protegés in the immediate post-War years: "Get the ball out to the wing *like lightning*!" Occasionally, situations arise today which call for the rapid transfer of the ball in similar fashion but now it may be a prop or a giant second-row forward waiting for the telling pass, hoping for the glory of being listed among the try-scorers.

In those far-off days when forwards needed to commit themselves and their opponents to the hurly-burly of maul and ruck, speedy wings had time and space. Not that they always needed either to outflank opposing defences for spectacular corner tries. At Murrayfield in 1971 Gerald Davies, on the right wing, formed an almost perfect arc as he ran around the Scottish cover defence to score in the right-hand corner. Left-footed kicker, flanker John Taylor, succeeded with the conversion from near the touchline to give Wales victory by 19 points to 18, thus remaining on course for a Grand Slam season.

Gerald Davies had the speed to outpace cover defences. He was also an outstanding exponent of the art of sidestepping, as befitted a player who began his senior rugby career as a centre (winning 11 Welsh caps in that position) and who had played some schoolboy rugby at outside-half. Add to these attributes his ability to swerve at pace and it is easy to see why he is recognised as one of the greatest wings. He may not have been capable of the bullocking runs which were the hallmark of Wales's left wing in the 1971 Grand Slam team, John Bevan, but Gerald Davies had all the other attributes of a finisher, vying with his contemporary, scrum-half Gareth Edwards, as leading Welsh

Ieuan Evans

international try-scorer. He played a key role in Wales's Grand Slam teams of 1971, 1976 and 1978 and film of his spectacular performance for the Lions against Hawke's Bay in 1971 is often brought down from the shelf to remind us of this most graceful and effective runner.

In more recent years, the exploits of Ieuan Evans, both for Llanelli and Wales in times of great adversity, marked him as a player deserving of every accolade in the game. He was the scorer of one of the most spectacular individual tries in rugby history, when with a succession of sidesteps he cleared several Scottish would-be tacklers at Cardiff. The look on Evans's face as he turned to his colleagues hinted at his own surprise. It was almost as though his brain couldn't fathom what his body had just achieved!

Several serious shoulder and ankle injuries notwithstanding, Ieuan Evans made 71 appearances for his country, scoring 33 tries and skippering his national team on 28 occasions, more than any other player to date. Had he been part of a successful team, as Gerald Davies was, we might well say that here was the greatest Welsh rugby hero. As it is, an occasional victory peppered an otherwise lean time for Wales. One such victory came in 1993 against England at Cardiff when the No. 8, Emyr Lewis, essayed an unlikely and speculative kick-ahead over the advancing defenders. Rory Underwood, an RAF pilot in a normal working day, but playing on England's left wing that afternoon, had somehow switched off his radar momentarily, allowing Ieuan Evans to win a kick-and-chase race and create a platform for a 10-9 Welsh victory.

A one-point victory against the old enemy was most welcome during a period of scant reward for loyal Welsh supporters. It was different from the Triple Crown-winning occasion at Cardiff in April 1969 when Maurice Richards, the Cardiff left wing, scored *four* tries as Wales thrashed England 30-9. Richards was an extremely talented winger whose defection to Rugby League made a large dent in the Welsh rugby armoury. Good fortune shone on the nation's rugby fortunes in the early 1970s with the arrival of another great left wing who set new standards of wing play in the red shirts of Llanelli, Wales and the Lions.

John J Williams (now remembered universally as 'J J') enjoyed a wonderful tour on the hard grounds of South Africa in 1974, scoring two tries in both the second and third Test matches to ensure a Lions series victory against the Springboks for the first time since 1896. His speed off the mark left opponents floundering as the Lions swept all before them. 1974 had promised to be a bad year for Williams when he claimed to have scored a try against England at Twickenham in March. I was sitting in the Ring seats at the North end of the old ground that day and I am as convinced as Williams that it was a perfectly good try. The referee, John West, in charge of his first International, did not agree and the men in white won the match 16-12. The singer, Max Boyce, was prompted to pen some verses about 'blind Irish referees' which is a little unfair on Mr West, although few Welshmen failed to notice that, in a year when Ireland won the Five Nations' Championship outright, if the try had been given, Wales would have shared the spoils with their Celtic cousins and with Phil Bennett's likely conversion would have won the match and the Championship.

J J Williams went on to enjoy spectacular success in the Grand Slam-winning teams of 1976 and 1978, the Triple Crown champions of 1977 and 1979 and as a member of the Lions team in New Zealand in 1977. Those Lions were only a whisker away from being as successful as their 1974 compatriots. J J scored the tourists' only try in their solitary Test victory against the All Blacks, as they lost a close series 3-1.

Williams was an excellent track sprinter before he devoted his time to rugby but his athletic achievements did not quite match those of an earlier wing. Ken J Jones achieved greatness on the right wing for Newport, Wales and the 1950 Lions in New Zealand and Australia. Jones's career spanned the years 1947-1957, his 44 Welsh caps far outstripping the previous record-holder, scrum-half R M (Dickie) Owen. Owen had played 35 times for his country between 1901 and 1912 including the first Welsh victory against the New Zealand All Blacks at Cardiff in 1905. Wales beat the All Blacks again in 1935 but have subsequently only managed one more victory over the Kiwis. The abiding memory from that later victorious match is of Ken Jones scoring a remarkable try to win against the All Blacks in 1953 at Cardiff Arms Park. Long-remembered for wing-forward Clem Thomas's cross-kick, it still needed Jones's electric pace to beat the cover defence.

Stuart Watkins, a tall and powerful wing from Newport, enjoyed one particular moment of glory in the 1966 encounter with France at Cardiff. Trailing 6-8 in the final stages of a close match, Wales looked as though they were about to concede another try as the French outside-half, Jean Gachassin, sliced through a gap on the Welsh 25-yard line to create a two-man overlap on the left. As the crowd held its collective breath, Watkins anticipated Gachassin's long, lobbed pass and effected a surprise interception. Looking 70 yards downfield, the opposing tryline must have seemed a whole universe away. French full-back, Claude Lacaze, twice came close to tackling Watkins, snapping at the heels of the tiring ball-carrier like an excitable terrier. Welsh supporters gasped as their hero's stride took him clear once, twice and over the line to win a breathtaking match by the narrowest of margins, nine points to eight. The bare statistics will never do justice to the excitement felt on the terraces that March day as in our minds we all ran each and every stride with Stuart Watkins.

When it came to speed and the holding of breath on terraces, nobody could match Nigel Walker's ability to produce a choral gasp from the crowd. A former Olympic sprint hurdler, Walker turned to rugby at an age when many would have already hung up their boots. His speed often took him away from would-be tacklers, particularly playing club rugby for Cardiff, but international defences were more organised and so space was usually at a premium. Walker would have achieved greatness had he played top class rugby in his 20s rather than pursuing a successful athletics career.

Among other Welsh wingers of the post-war years, Dewi Bebb stands out. He scored the winning try on his debut against England at Cardiff in 1959. Bebb, playing on the left wing throughout his international career, went on to score both tries in a 6-3 victory in the corresponding match two years later. The English points were scored by the man marking Bebb that January day, Olympic sprinter John Young. Several other fliers promised but failed to achieve greatness. Ray Williams, Robert Morgan and Wayne Proctor, all of Llanelli, performed brilliantly at times for their club, as did W K M Jones and Adrian Hadley for Cardiff. Welsh rugby has produced its fair share of wingers; with a few worthy exceptions, however, they have flown past in a twinkling without attaining heroic status. Sadly for Wales, other than Hadley's outstanding performance in scoring two tries against England in the 1988 Triple Crown-winning team, no recent player has consistently emulated the feats of Ken Jones, Stuart Watkins, Gerald Davies, J J Williams and Ieuan Evans.

Gerald Davies

When Welsh rugby was riding the crest of a wave in the 1970s, threequarters like Ray Gravell of Llanelli supposedly ate soft centres! A succession of centres had to bow to the combination of skill and force embodied in players like Gravell.

Just as Barry John achieved the ultimate accolade in being hailed 'King' John by his many admirers, so Wales had, in an earlier age, produced the 'Prince' of centres. Bleddyn Williams has vied with Gareth Edwards in a variety of readers' polls to name the Greatest Welsh rugby player of all time. Legend has it that Bleddyn Williams, one of eight brothers who grew up in the village of Taffs Well some seven miles north of Cardiff, learned his basic rugby skills by playing with an old shoe wrapped in newspaper. Like so many players of his era, the Second World War postponed the start of Williams's international career but as soon as hostilities ceased, he made his mark in the so-called Victory Internationals. In the Victory International against France at Swansea in December 1945, Bleddyn Williams gave a sparse crowd of Welsh supporters a foretaste of what was to come with a scintillating display, culminating in a brilliant midfield break to give fellow-centre Jack Matthews a try. Another superb Williams break, followed by a pinpoint crosskick, paved the way for a forwards' try and the conversion, firmly establishing Wales as a major force in post-war rugby.

An automatic choice for his country until his retirement in 1955, Bleddyn Williams won 22 caps and would have been first choice to captain Wales to the Grand Slams of 1950 and 1952 had injury and illness not kept him off the field. His misfortune paved the way for forward John Gwilliam to establish himself as a leader without peer among Welsh rugby players. Williams, however, was selected as vice-captain of Karl Mullen's 1950 Lions and is unique among Welsh rugby players in having, in 1953, led his club and his

Ray Gravell

country to victory against the All Blacks. Even in adversity, Bleddyn Williams was a player great enough to shine, most notably when Wales lost to Ireland at Belfast in 1948. Despite ferocious Irish tackling in midfield that day, Williams made several telling breaks, but the support was never at his shoulder when he needed it. In the end, the only Welsh score came from Bleddyn Williams breaking and cutting back inside the Irish cover for a solo try. It was a day when the 'Prince' was in his pomp and the courtiers around really were barely fit to lace his boots.

New Zealander Graham Henry was dubbed 'The Great Redeemer' when he arrived to coach the Welsh national team at the end of the 1990s. Bleddyn Williams had been truly 'The Great Provider' when it came to playing skills. His partnership, for club and country, with Jack Matthews, raised Welsh rugby to a level rarely seen before or since. Although they shared only three international victories for their country, they made a formidable pairing in New Zealand and Australia with the 1950 Lions. Any youngster growing up in South Wales in the 1950s was steeped in the history of, "Bleddyn, who sliced through opposition defences at will and Jack, the greatest crash-tackler the game has ever seen." Even now, in the days of 'big hits' and drift defences, these two rugby wizards would have thrilled the crowds with their innate skills and cavalier attitude. Sadly though, professionalism might have stifled their devil-may-care style of rugby.

On that 1950 Lions tour, as Williams and Matthews provided opportunities for wing Ken Jones, an already experienced young man was waiting to play a dominant role in the centre for Wales throughout the 1950s. Malcolm Thomas had been capped in 1949 while serving as a young Navy Officer and was to be the mainstay of the Newport and Wales threequarter line for the following ten years. Injury and loss of form deprived him of the opportunity of touring with the 1955 Lions in South Africa, where the hard grounds might have enabled him to demonstrate his range of skills. Malcolm Thomas was durable enough to return to the Antipodes with the Lions in 1959 where he operated in the shadow of truly great centres – Englishman Jeff Butterfield, David Hewitt from Ireland and fellow-Welshman, Malcolm Price of Pontypool.

Williams and Matthews proved particularly difficult acts for centres such as Gareth Griffiths, Gordon Wells (both of Cardiff) and Cyril Davies (Llanelli) to follow. While Malcolm Thomas was a solid player throughout the decade, Wales needed the sparkle which Cyril Davies displayed for his club. Sadly, a severe knee injury cut short what might have been an exciting career. Malcolm Price appeared to be the answer to the nation's prayers as he vied with Butterfield and Hewitt on tour with the 1959 Lions but the lure of cash proved too much for the Gwent man and he turned to Rugby League.

Another Gwent centre earned a place in the history books on a murky mid-week afternoon in the autumn of 1963 as the touring All Blacks went down to their only defeat in a 36-match tour of Britain, France and Canada. J R (Dick) Uzzell's drop-goal for Newport was the only score in that match and, although he only played five times for his country, he was an important part of the Triple Crown team of 1965. Uzzell's co-centre in 1965 was the young John Dawes and they were seen as a functional rather than an exciting midfield pairing. Missing that season through injury was a product of the fly-half factory at Gwendraeth Grammar School, who had been converted into a particularly exciting runner at centre. D K (Ken) Jones had been acknowledged from his schooldays as one of the most exciting runners of his day with an innate ability to jink and swerve at speed. Touring with the Lions in South Africa in 1962 and Australia and New Zealand in 1966, Jones proved that he could hold his own with the best attacking players of his generation. The contemptuous ease with which he beat opponents matched other products of Gwendraeth, such as Carwyn James, Barry John, Gareth Davies and Jonathan Davies. An Oxford Blue who later carved out a successful business career, Ken Jones was an enigma who performed brilliantly at the highest level. He was undoubtedly a hero in his playing days, setting crowds alight with his electrifying pace and, but for injury, studies and his desire to pursue a career outside the game, might have achieved a status almost equal to that of Bleddyn Williams.

Another player from West Wales who changed position, this time from centre to wing, and might have achieved true greatness as a centre, was Gerald Davies. His exploits on the wing for Wales and the Lions are mentioned elsewhere but he would be among the first to acknowledge his good fortune in playing outside several exceptional centres throughout his career. Having made the switch to wing in 1971, Gerald Davies fed off the quick ball passed along the threequarter line prompted by his club captain, John Dawes, who led Wales to a Grand Slam that year and then steered the Lions to a 2-1 series victory against the All Blacks on their home soil. Dawes was not a demonstrative player, rarely able to make a telling midfield break at the highest level, but he was blessed with an innate ability to pass the ball accurately, swiftly and, when required to do so, in one movement of taking and giving the ball. When a centre is able to perform these skills at speed, as John Dawes was during his later career, the players around him can prosper and beat defences almost at will.

The whole of Wales worried when Dawes retired from international rugby after the 1971 Lions tour, but two former pupils from Gerald Davies's old school, Carmarthen Boys' Grammar School, stepped into the breach. Roy Bergiers, a young Welshman of Belgian extraction, began his international career playing against England in January 1972 but achieved his own moment of glory when he charged down full-back Joe Karam's clearance kick and scored the try which enabled the Llanelli club to beat the 1972 touring All Blacks.

Alongside Bergiers that day was the even younger Ray Gravell, the Welshman who, above all others, still wears his rugby heart most conspicuously on his sleeve. Bergiers and Gravell became Lions, the former playing second fiddle to Dick Milliken of Ireland and the Scot, Ian McGeechan, on the ultra-

Scott Gibbs

successful 1974 tour of South Africa. Gravell played in all four Tests against the 'Boks with Bill Beaumont's 1980 tourists. He formed an extremely successful partnership with Steve Fenwick of Bridgend in the late 1970s, at the heart of the Grand Slam seasons of 1976 and 1978. When you throw in the Triple Crowns of 1977 and 1979, it is immediately apparent that they achieved more in terms of results than even Bleddyn Williams himself. Gravell was acknowledged as one of the most powerful centres of his day, tackling ferociously and often requiring more than one opponent to bring him down when he embarked on a charging run. Fenwick had the added skills of a successful goalkicker but his silky running and smooth passing showed that he had all the requisite qualities for greatness in midfield.

Wales has waited patiently for the same level of success as in those far-off heady 1970 days. The nation was led to its only Triple Crown since 1979 by a Swansea centre, Bleddyn Bowen. His mid-field partner that day was Mark Ring, a magical player who readily opened his box of tricks to entertain the crowd. Sometimes ignoring the fact that he was wearing boots, 'Ringo' earned a notoriety for unorthodox kicks-ahead, bouncing the ball on his thigh or knee, a perfectly legitimate ploy which sometimes confused opponents and referees. During a lean time for Welsh rugby, Mark Ring was an entertainer of the highest order, the ball often disappearing behind his back as he kidded opponents he had already passed it.

Even when victories were sparse, Welsh centres continued to slice through opposition defences or take out opposing tacklers to free support runners who scored the occasional exciting try. One particular try will live in the collective Welsh memory for many years to come, both for its audacity and crucial timing and also as it deprived the Old Enemy, England, of a Grand Slam season. Wales had played two seasons of international rugby at the home of English soccer, Wembley Stadium, by the time they faced England themselves in the shadow of the Twin Towers, in April 1999. The white-shirted strong men were thought to believe that they need only turn up to secure the victory which would crown them as the undisputed rugby champions of the Northern Hemisphere.

They had, however, reckoned without the strength of Wales's most potent mid-field force of the previous decade. True, it was largely Neil Jenkins's right boot which had kept Wales in the game but the ultimate glory of securing a successful farewell to Wembley for Wales rests with Scott Gibbs. Gibbs's ferocious tackling contributed hugely to the Lions' success in winning the Test series in South Africa in 1997 and he was always capable of breaking the strongest midfield defences with his powerful running. Indeed, his performance was a key element in Swansea's win against World Champions, Australia, at St Helen's in 1992. 1999 however, was something different. England were known for their big-hitting tacklers and with only one try, by full-back Shane Howarth, to show for their afternoon's work, victory seemed an impossible task for Wales.

Gibbs, however, had other ideas. He barged his way past ineffectual English tackling and jinked around flailing arms before raising his own arm in triumph as he crossed the line. Wales were still one point behind and, just as at Murrayfield 28 years previously, many were too nervous to watch Neil Jenkins's successful conversion. A victory by one point, 32-31, secured Scott Gibbs's place among the very greatest of Welsh rugby heroes.

10: OUTSIDE-HALF

When Arwel Thomas made his international debut against Italy on a cold January evening in 1996, someone sitting near me in the North Stand at Cardiff Arms Park remarked that the Welsh outside-half factory had been cranked into action again. "After several years of rusty redundancy," he added as an afterthought.

The fact that Neil Jenkins was already breaking all sorts of records wearing the No. 10 shirt meant nothing to this particular fan. He was in thrall to the notion that a Welsh international fly-half should be a dancing magician, who can weave spells to outwit and outscore the opposition.

The fact that we have two names for the wearer of the No. 10 shirt encapsulates the problem in assessing the merits of various players.

The diminutive fly-half is seen by many as different to the (usually) stockier outside-half, even though they are, on the field, one and the same. The Antipodeans call him the first five-eighth. The French use the word '*ouvert*' to imply a role as an 'opener-up' of the play.

In making any assessment of the merits of the various No. 10s for Wales, it has, therefore, to be borne in mind that fly-halves must occasionally adopt the guise of a 'tenth forward' (see *9: Scrum-Half*). Some players, notably Neil Jenkins, have encompassed each and every role required of the No. 10, while others have relied on their innate skills and star quality in some areas while relying on others to fulfil the other (sometimes) mundane tasks.

Some truly heroic Welsh fly-halves, such as David Watkins, Phil Bennett, Jonathan Davies and, in a slightly earlier age, Cliff Ashton, seemed far too small to survive the grittiness of rugby on a wet, muddy pitch. Barry John, in his pomp, appeared to look disdainfully at fellow-players who actually muddied their shirts.

Cliff Morgan, the star Wales and Lions outside-half throughout my

Neil Jenkins

childhood, managed to embody the dancing nonchalance of the will-o'-the-wisp fly-half with a degree of hardness which earned the admiration of friend and foe alike. His crouching gait often surprised opposing wing-forwards and swiftly put him beyond their reach. Two notable examples of Morgan's teeth-gritting determination to reach the try-line occurred in 1955, truly an annus mirabilis for him.

Against Ireland at Cardiff in March 1955 he wrong-footed, among others, the great Irish three-quarter, Tony O'Reilly, to score a solo try, inspiring Wales to turn a likely 3-3 draw into an amazing 21-3 victory. A few weeks later, on tour in South Africa with the British Lions, on receiving the ball from a set-piece, Morgan put his head back and outpaced the aggressive Springbok defender, Basie van Wyk, leading his team to victory by 23-22 in one of the greatest rugby international matches of all time.

Cliff Morgan made the No.10 shirt his own in the mid-1950s, much to the chagrin of Llanelli Rugby Club supporters. Their hero of the day was one Carwyn James, who eventually won two Welsh international caps, the second as centre against France in March 1958. He later achieved greatness as a coach, masterminding a series victory for the Lions in New Zealand in 1971 and a stunning triumph for Llanelli against the All Blacks in October 1972. I had the privilege of being taught by Carwyn for eight years and of being tormented (as an aspiring schoolboy wing-forward) by his seeming ability to disappear just as I launched into a tackle!

Carwyn James was educated at Gwendraeth Grammar School, set amongst the spoil heaps of the local anthracite mines. This school truly was the fly-half factory of modern fable, producing within a quarter of a century, under the tutelage of Ray Williams, D Ken Jones (who, although a successful schoolboy fly-half, was to achieve fame as a centre for Wales and the Lions), Barry John, Gareth Davies and Jonathan Davies.

Barry John achieved the ultimate accolade 'The King' following huge personal success with Carwyn's 1971 Lions. It would be churlish to claim that this monarch of the rugby pitch needed coaching. Gareth Davies also achieved stunning success with Wales and the Lions, touring South Africa with Bill Beaumont's 1980 squad later. He established himself as an administrator of note, leading BBC Wales's Sports Department before becoming Chief Executive of Cardiff Rugby Club and later heading up the Sports Council for Wales.

Barry John

Jonathan Davies, like David Watkins a quarter of a century earlier, played in a Triple Crown-winning team. Great things were expected from both of these players but they 'went North' to join the professional game of Rugby League. They certainly succeeded there but many Rugby Union purists were saddened that their greatest achievements came in the 13-a-side game. Both returned to Wales, Watkins to become Chief Executive of Newport RFC, where he had first achieved fame, and Davies to play a couple of seasons back in the Union game with Cardiff before becoming a radio and television commentator, covering Union and League for the BBC.

Watkins, despite his sojourn in Rugby League, has remained loyal to Newport RFC while Jonathan Davies starred for Neath and Llanelli and, at the end of his career, for Cardiff. Barry John moved from Llanelli to play for Cardiff while Neil Jenkins left his beloved Pontypridd for the Capital City club. Many felt that Gareth Davies's spiritual home was Stradey Park, home of Llanelli, but this particular Gwendraeth product also chose to play his rugby in Cardiff.

Some rugby supporters in England were bemused to see Gareth Davies's name in Welsh teams in the late 1970s and 1980s as they thought he had already retired. Another Gareth Davies, also a product of the Gwendraeth fly-half factory, had starred for Bedford RFC a decade earlier and held, for many years, the club's record for the number of drop-goals scored in a season. This Gareth Davies did not become a rugby hero in his homeland but is still remembered with great respect at Goldington Road.

James, Watkins, John, Gareth Davies (the international) and Jonathan Davies were all adroit drop-kickers but I shall always remember the young Phil Bennett, even as a schoolboy, being able to change the course of a game with a sudden drop-goal. Accurate kicking has always been a hallmark of a great fly-half although one or two post-war Welsh players, notably Billy Cleaver and Brian Richards, relied too heavily on putting boot to ball, restricting their backs' opportunities to run with the ball.

It was his ability to play an attacking game from all corners of the pitch which marked Phil Bennett's rugby. He, like Cliff Morgan, Barry John and others, often performed seeming miracles for his country but the one abiding memory I have of his attacking prowess was for Llanelli against Bath on a bitterly cold December Saturday.

Taking the ball under his own posts following a scrum and running from right to left from the Pwll End at Stradey Park, all of us on the 'Tanner Bank' assumed that Bennett would kick downfield to clear his lines. He gleefully shovelled the ball on to his inside centre, Gwyn Ashby, as though he wished to pass on the responsibilty to his colleague. Before Ashby had had time to think, his fly-half had run round behind him and appeared outside him ready to take the pass. Ashby duly passed and everyone in the ground was amazed to see Bennett shoot through the narrow gap between the Bath centres.

He ran towards the left-hand touchline as though it was a race to be first to the flag on the half-way line. The covering defenders appeared on a collision course but Bennett had other ideas. The true mark of his greatness was that, in effect, he did *nothing*! He just stopped dead in his tracks and watched as several defenders stumbled over the touchline, having failed even to touch their quarry. As soon as he was satisfied that his path was clear, the little fly-half darted onwards on a diagonal run to score an unopposed try under the posts. Although simple in its execution, with no jinking, sidestepping or swerving, this try remains just about the most spectacular I have seen.

The sheer cheek and devilry of the archetypical Welsh fly-half were encapsulated in the few seconds it took Phil Bennett to fashion and score this try. It is, indeed, the benchmark against which I measure all other tries. Yes, there have been other great tries scored by backs and forwards but it is the one event which, for me, elevates 'Benny' from little Felinfoel to a higher status as a Welsh rugby hero than all our other Welsh fly-halves.

Many scrum-halves, over the years, have been called the 'ninth forward', implying a secondary role behind the pack as it grinds the opposition down. Others were seen as a link to provide the ball, hard-won by the forwards, on a plate ready for the nippy backs to show their paces. A third group of skilful runners could prise open the meanest defence almost at will.

Few players have managed to combine all three roles effectively. Although a number of extremely able players have played at scrum-half for Wales, most have been specialists, mastering only one or two of the necessary skills.

Since the Second World War, battle-hardened exponents of scrum-half play have worn the scarlet shirt of Wales, with Clive Rowlands box-kicking his country to a Triple Crown in 1965 as the highlight of an otherwise barren period. Rowlands's son-in-law, Robert Jones, brought similar kicking prowess to the position, allied to a swift, long pass, but in spite of occasional individual breaches of opposition defensive lines, Jones did not have the killer instinct of a great try-scoring finisher. In the '90s, there emerged a particularly talented and powerful player, Rob Howley, but possibly because recent changes in the game have given rise to blanket defensive patterns, he failed to reach the starry heights of his predecessors before the turn of the century.

Thought by many to have been the most inventive of scrum-halves, particularly as the co-instigator (with M J K Smith, his outside-half partner at Oxford University, who played in one international match for England but who achieved fame as an England cricket captain) of the scissors-pass, Onllwyn Brace constantly mesmerised opponents at club level with a bottomless bag of tricks. At international level, however, defences were more alert and sophisticated and invariably stifled a player who was as close to

Gareth Edwards

genius as any scrum-half has ever been.

For many years, the most-capped Welsh international rugby player was a scrum-half at the height of his powers in the early 1900s . R M (Dickie) Owen represented his country on 35 occasions including the famous victory against the first touring All Blacks in 1905. Like most players in the position, Owen was an exceptionally tough character for his size and set an exacting standard for those who followed.

Haydn Tanner, who played for both Swansea and Cardiff, wore the red of Wales on 25 occasions and is still held by many to be the greatest of all Welsh No.9s. Tanner's international career spanned the years before and after the Second World War. As a young schoolboy in 1936, he played in a winning team against the touring New Zealanders but, sadly, in spite of his great achievements, the best years of his playing ability were lost to the war. Tanner was a truly great player and might be considered 'the greatest' scrum-half had his career run its full course and had an equally precocious young player from west Wales not appeared on the scene in the late 1960s.

Gareth Owen Edwards grew up in the mining village of Gwauncae-gurwen, showing such exceptional sporting talent that he won a sports scholarship to Millfield School. Saddened though he was by the loss of such a gem of a player, Edwards's PE teacher at Pontardawe Secondary School in the Swansea Valley, Bill Samuel, had nurtured the boy to do nothing less than play for Wales. Samuel acknowledged that it was in Edwards's interest to move to what has long been recognised as a centre of sporting excellence.

Like J P R Williams, Gareth Edwards benefitted from his time at Millfield and many thought that the player was ready to play for his country against John Thornett's touring Wallabies in December 1966, having played only a handful of first-class matches. But the newly-returned British Lion, Alan Lewis of Abertillery, was preferred to partner debutant Barry John and Wales were beaten in a close match. Edwards had to wait until the spring to make his debut against France in Paris and retained his place to play a supporting role in 'Jarrett's Match' (April 1967 see *15: Full Back*). For the next ten years, however, he was the scrum-half who ruled the roost at No.9 for Wales, the Lions and the Barbarians while making fewer and fewer appearances in the Blue and Black of Cardiff.

In those pre-professional days, Edwards saw playing for his country as the utmost priority, causing much frustration to club supporters both in Cardiff and elsewhere. Occasionally large numbers of supporters, particularly at away matches, were given the disappointing last-minute news that the great Gareth Edwards would not be playing that afternoon. A tweaked hamstring or some such was often tendered as the reason for the great man's absence but supporters, particularly among English clubs, couldn't help but notice that Edwards never missed a game for his country through injury. Amateur players were, to some extent, able to pick and choose which matches to play and had Gareth Edwards not rationed his appearances, his career might have been curtailed. Having built a successful partnership with Barry John in the late 1960s and early 1970s, Edwards became even more successful in tandem with Phil Bennett in the later 1970s, probably thanks to his shrewdness in selecting which matches to play.

Gareth Edwards left one indelible mark on rugby which has influenced all later players at all levels of the game. The modern torpedo spinning pass was first perfected in the Northern Hemisphere by the young Edwards, although many credit the great All Black scrum-half, Chris Laidlaw, with its invention. After the Lions tour of South Africa in 1968, when injury restricted Edwards to two of the four Tests, Cardiff supporters waited expectantly at the start of the new season. Rumour had it that Gareth Edwards had doubled, trebled or even quadrupled the length of his pass. And it would not be a dive-pass. Scrum-halves down the ages had fallen into the trap of reducing their team, albeit momentarily, by one as they belly-flopped for extra passing length trying to free their fly-half from marauding wing-forwards.

To gasps of astonishment, Gareth Edwards revealed his 'new' pass during a mid-week home match against Newport and, like most supporters who witnessed the extra freedom enjoyed by Barry John that evening, I knew that here was the scrum-half genius for whom Wales had waited. Edwards's exploits merit volumes, such was the presence of the man on the rugby field. He was held in such high esteem at the end of the Millennium that a variety of polls hailed him as the greatest Welsh rugby player of all time. While it will always be difficult to compare players of differing eras, particularly with the advent of the professional game, there is no doubting the achievements of Gareth Edwards.

Most people will remember him for that inimitable injection of pace which put him on the end of the incredible movement for the Barbarians against the All Blacks at Cardiff in 1973. Many will also realise that Edwards, in effect, poached wing John Bevan's try. The scrum-half's ability to get himself into a position to do such poaching brought him 20 tries for his country. In the days when flankers were far less restricted than in the modern professional game, this was an astonishing total for an 'inside-half' (another alternative title for the position).

Terry Holmes, of whom great things had been expected, succeeded Edwards to the No. 9 shirt for club, country and Lions. He never really lived up to expectations, partly because of injury but also because he was not, in the final analysis, as rounded a player as Edwards. Holmes burst on the scene in 1978 as spectacularly as Gareth Edwards had done a dozen years earlier. Showing remarkably similar promise, Holmes carried the hopes of a nation on his broad shoulders. He was a member of a Triple Crown-winning team in 1979, his first season of Five Nations rugby, and went with the 1980 Lions to South Africa. He formed a more than able half-back partnership in tandem with Gareth Davies for club and country before the financial lure of Rugby League ended his Union playing career. Terry Holmes later returned to the Union game as a successful coach with the Cardiff club. It seems fitting that he spent the year 2000 at the capital city club when Gareth Edwards was a member of the club's board of directors, overseeing its transition into the professional age. With Robert Howley operating at the base of the scrum and as Haydn Tanner ended his playing days in the blue and black shirt, Cardiff can truly claim to have had the real scrum-half heroes of late 20th century Welsh rugby among its ranks.

Robert Howley

As Welsh rugby struggled to cope with the professional era, one player with all the attributes to be a great No.8 appeared on the verge of fulfilling his early promise. With his father Derek's build and the great Welsh outside-half Barry John his uncle, Scott Quinnell had a pedigree second to none in Welsh rugby (apart from his younger brother, Craig, with whom he has played for Llanelli, Richmond and Wales). Pedigree counts for nothing, however, and promise is worthless unless a player applies himself fully.

Scott Quinnell promised much in his early 20s. He scored such a powerful solo try from the back of a line-out against France at Cardiff in 1994 that Welsh supporters were hailing the event as the dawn of a new era even before the young man had showered away the liniment from his aching muscles and downed a celebratory shandy. The advent of the professional game was a few months too late to stop Quinnell following the cash-strewn path to Rugby League with St Helens but he eventually returned, first with Richmond and then back to his home-town club, Llanelli. Captaincy of both club and country takes Scott a step further than father Derek and, had the son been blessed with as safe a pair of hands as his father or, better still, had father and son had as safe hands as Mervyn Davies's, greatness indeed might have been thrust upon both generations of back-row forwards.

Derek Quinnell, as he tried to break into the Welsh team in the early 1970s, had to stand in the shadow of greatness, as he understudied Mervyn Davies, truly the best Welsh No. 8 of the modern era. Whereas Derek Quinnell had been groomed by Llanelli to play for Wales, Mervyn Davies appeared from nowhere (if junior club rugby in Surrey equates with 'nowhere'!) just in time for London Welsh's 1968 Christmas tour of South

Mervyn Davies

Wales. The lean former Swansea student got his hands on the No.8 shirt, sharing a debut victory with full-back J P R Williams against Scotland at Murrayfield the following February. Compared to many beefy forwards, Davies's spare frame, the dark hair always encased in a white bandage, seemed at times too frail for top-class rugby.

In Mervyn Davies, however, Wales found itself the most complete back-row forward of his day and possibly of all time. Almost spider-like in his ability to snare opposing ball-carriers close to scrum and line-out, his huge stride took him around the field as quickly as some of the faster threequarters. Invariably ripping away opposition ball or rapidly recycling his own team's possession, Davies was often the unnoticed instigator of try-producing movements which, at inception, seemed doomed to failure. Reigning supreme at the back of the line-out and adept at making timely breaks from the back of the scrum, here was a true master of the science of No. 8 play.

An integral part of Wales's success in the early 1970s, Mervyn Davies was a cornerstone of the Lions successful tours of New Zealand in 1971 and of South Africa in 1974. Having captained Wales to a Grand Slam in 1976, he was seen as the natural choice to lead the Lions to New Zealand the following year but a sub-arachnoid haemorrhage suffered during a Welsh Cup semi-final in Cardiff, however, ended his brilliant career. His tragic illness deprived the Lions of an inspirational captain and ended Davies's personal goal of winning three Grand Slams in successive years. Even without him, Wales succeeded in winning a further Grand Slam in 1978 and the winning of four successive Triple Crowns, in 1976, 1977, 1978 and 1979, showed the depth of talent available to Wales during that time.

The great Abertillery and Wales No. 8 of the 1960s, Alun Pask, had a great knack for the unexpected. Carrying the ball in one hand, sometimes high above his head in readiness to throw it to left or right to a supporting

Scott Quinnell

player, marked him out as the most Fijian-like player of his day. The famous photograph of Pask in an arcing dive over a diminutive Western Province defender when on tour with the 1962 Lions in South Africa, showed his ability to think and act at speed. Such skills were more in keeping with the fleet-footed backs than the 'donkey' forwards. Pask had not been a certainty for selection for the 1962 Lions but, in that year's Wales-v-France match at Cardiff, he showed his pace by catching Henri Rancoule to help secure a 3-0 victory for Wales. Many observers ruefully admitted that the No. 8's tackle on the La Rochelle wing would win Pask a place on the tour even though, on balance, his form over the season had not justified his selection. Pask seized his chance and developed into a great hero even though his only major team success was with Clive Rowlands's Triple Crown winners in 1965.

Wales had stuck with the old 3-2-3 scrum formation in the years following the Second World War, even though modern thinking accepted that 3-4-1, leaving the No. 8 as the sole backrower, was more efficient. Players such as Russell Robins and John Faull, at their peak under the 3-2-3 system, were able, occasionally, to coast around the field, knowing that the speedier flankers would cover the ground. David Nash and Glyn Davidge, like Pask both strong men of Gwent, were ready to roam to all corners of the field. Later exponents of the art of No. 8 play, such as Jeff Squire, Eddie Butler, Phil Davies (who was a better second row than No. 8), Emyr Lewis and Stuart Davies each made a brief impression, with Squire making his mark as a Lion in 1977 and 1980. Squire had the good fortune to play his club rugby behind the famous Pontypool front row and alongside flanker Terry Cobner.

Although Emyr Lewis never quite achieved all that he promised, he has the distinction that his nickname while playing for Llanelli, '*Tarw*' ('Bull'), gave rise to the Welsh expression '*llwybr tarw*' for the thundering path beaten by hefty forwards as they crash into opponents. Sadly though, however much bullocking running their No. 8s have made in the last years of the 20th century, the other rugby-playing nations have had their own stars who have, by and large, eclipsed whoever Wales could throw into the fray. Although sometimes criticised for a lack of fitness and an unsafe pair of hands, Scott Quinnell has a natural talent approaching that of Mervyn Davies.

While the younger Quinnell had not quite achieved greatness in the 20th century, the first Lions tour of the new Millennium to Australia at last saw the emergence of a great Welsh No. 8 hero to challenge Davies's achievments.

A wily, wiry and particularly nippy little fly-half was once heard to remark that he only worried if he could 'smell the flanker's liniment'. The duel between one team's half-backs and the opposition wing-forwards (as flankers have been known down the ages) is at the heart of Rugby Union and, whatever developments are brought to the game, ardent followers will still revel in this bullfight-like contest-within-a-contest. The charging, often bullocking flanker sees the half-backs as prey while their elusive and usually smaller opponents dance on their tiptoes and are gone from the forward's grasp in an instant.

An early post-war exponent of the art of wing-forward play was deemed too tough to tour with the 1950 Lions 'Down Under'. Ray Cale of Pontypool set the standard for many hard Gwent forwards to follow and won seven Welsh caps in 1949 and 1950. Every fly-half who played against him told stories of how he always snared them early in a match and how they were rarely able to use the ball constructively after that. Had Cale not been so callously ignored by the Lions selectors, we might revere him now as the greatest Welsh flanker of all time. As it is, with so few memories of him, he is largely forgotten in any analysis of players from the side of the scrum.

The player who succeeded Ray Cale achieved his greatest fame for being at the heart of one of the most important tries in Welsh rugby history. R C C (Clem) Thomas played in 26 matches for his country but will always be remembered for his audacious cross-kick which provided Ken Jones, playing on the right wing, with the winning try against the 1953 touring New Zealanders. Wales have beaten New Zealand three times in all, only once in the second half of the 20th century. At the beginning of a new Millennium, it appears less and less likely that we will see a Welsh team emulate the Welsh teams of 1905, 1936 and 1953 in defeating the All Blacks. In placing his cross-kick in Ken Jones's path on that cold December day almost half a century ago, Clem

John Taylor

Thomas achieved a greatness which few other flankers have since matched.

Clem Thomas was not only the scourge of opposing fly-halves and an occasionally adept cross-kicker. He was, as has always been required of the flank forward, usually first at the breakdown of a movement, able to recycle possession (before the term had been invented) to set his backs away again swiftly. Thomas became, despite injury early on the tour, an integral part of the Lions party in South Africa in 1955 and set a high standard for others to follow. That others have succeeded in approaching his achievement says much for the quality of wing-forwards produced by Welsh clubs over the years.

Haydn Morgan of Abertillery also played 26 times for his country, including the 1965 Triple Crown season, and toured with the 1959 and 1962 Lions. His all-embracing tackles on opposition backs often provided clubmate and international colleague, Alun Pask, with valuable possession. Like Clem Thomas, Haydn Morgan was always at the heart of Welsh attacks, supporting his colleagues. Many pundits of Morgan's era suggested that he could have been an equally effective centre-threequarter at international level. His versatility would indeed have enabled him to play in a variety of positions.

Despite Clem Thomas's adroitness at cross-kicking and Haydn Morgan's all-round rugby skills, neither could count top-class goalkicking in their personal armoury. John Taylor, a member of the great London Welsh team of the late 1960s and early 1970s, was a left-footed place-kicker of the highest class. His ice-cool nervelessness enabled Wales to win a match at Murrayfield in 1971 which had appeared lost beyond redemption. Gerald Davies raced in for a great try far out near the right touchline bringing Wales within a point of their opponents. The conversion was still required for victory. Few players or spectators were able to bear watching Taylor as he placed the ball ever so casually and swiftly kicked it between the posts to keep his team's Grand Slam aspirations on course.

John Taylor, a product of Watford Boys' Grammar School, was a young man whose mother had instilled into her son an undying loyalty towards

Welsh rugby. His international career started by accident as a result of a bloody collision during his club's traditional Boxing Day fixture against Llanelli in 1966. His head swathed in yards of white bandage on a gloomy Stradey Park December day, Taylor was to be seen everywhere, tackling, restarting dying movements, rucking, mauling, sprinting with the fastest threequarters and (according to one excitable wag on the old Tanner bank) he was "probably reinventing the wheel in the middle of a ruck!" Those of us fortunate enough to be at St Helen's the following day, watching the Exiles play against Swansea, knew instinctively, on seeing that bandaged head appear at the forefront of all the action again, that we were witnessing the start of an illustrious career.

By 1971, John Taylor was a fixture in the national team, having toured South Africa with the 1968 Lions. He had the moral courage to refuse to play for his country against the touring Springboks at the end of 1969 to express his solidarity with anti-Apartheid protesters who disrupted the tour.

Taylor played a number of international matches with his fellow London Welshman, Mervyn Davies, at No. 8 and the incomparable Dai Morris of Neath on the blindside flank of the scrum. Morris played much of his club rugby at No. 8 and understood the requirements of all three back-row positions better than most. At times revelling in the nickname 'Shadow', Dai Morris seemed to appear from nowhere to smother-tackle opponents and provide his colleagues with much-needed ball when all seemed lost. As the South Wales coalfield contracted in the 1960s, Dai Morris was one of a dying breed of international players. A colliery fitter for most of the week, he plied his flanker's trade on match day with a gritty strength which few of his contemporaries had any hope of matching. One of the sadnesses of this hero's playing career was that he was never selected to tour with the Lions. According to fans' conjecture at the Gnoll, the Lions selectors recognised that Dai Morris could not really afford to take time off from his normal work to indulge in an amateur tour lasting three or four months. How different from the professional era now.

Earlier in the 1960s, another hard man of the blind side, Gary Prothero, had come up through the ranks at Bridgend to play an integral part in the 1965 Triple Crown-winning team and to tour with the 1966 Lions. Described by some as lacking in charisma, Prothero was every bit as tough as Dai Morris and bottled up the blind side for any marauding opposition scrum-half.

While one or two players specialised in playing on the blind side, others have been pitched into the role to stop specific opponents. Derek Quinnell, normally a No. 8, was selected in the role for one Test on the 1971 Lions tour with the specific task of preventing New Zealand scrum-half Sid Going from playing his normal game. So successful was Quinnell that he was promptly dropped, on the basis that the All Blacks would have now rumbled the ploy and so a new strategy was required.

The versatility of players such as Derek Quinnell, able to switch between back-row positions, has meant that some flankers have been quite happy to play on a right and left basis rather than open and blind. Colin Charvis epitomises this. Coupled with his willingness to perform equally well at No. 8, the Swansea forward brings an abrasiveness to Welsh forward play which has earned him praise from all quarters.

Charvis suffered the indignity of being banned from two games during the 1999 World Cup following what the tournament administrators saw as violent play. The line between acceptable aggression and outright violence on the rugby field is a very fine one and flankers invariably find themselves close to the wrong side of it. From Ray Cale in the early post-war years to Colin Charvis at the end of the century, referees and administrators have the problem of how to balance the aggressive force of the bulky, yet swift, flanker and the usually diminutive, elusive, half-back. One player, more than most, who was cast in the role of villain, while seen as a hero in Wales, was Paul Ringer. Ringer was certainly an aggressive tackler who saw to it that few, if any, opposing fly-halves made any headway against him. His sending off at Twickenham in 1980 was seen by many Welsh supporters as pre-judged. The media had hyped his aggressive style so much that referees were keeping him firmly in their sights. Sadly for Ringer, his late tackle on the England flyhalf, John Horton, was rightly seen as outside the law. He compounded the tackle's lateness by extending his hand and fingers towards the Englishman in such a way that Irish referee, David Burnett, had little choice but to send Ringer from the field. Subsequently lionised by many of his compatriots for subduing Horton until the sending-off, Paul Ringer was never again able to achieve the level of controlled aggression required to achieve true greatness.

Aggression is part and parcel of a flanker's makeup. He constantly strives to show opposing half-backs that he rules the play. It is, therefore, surprising to find that, from time to time, Welsh rugby has thrown up flankers who have combined aggression with a grace more associated with lithe threequarters. This trait was personified in Haydn Morgan and Clem Thomas. John Taylor was an ungainly yet effective runner. Other players who had a wide range of the flanker's essential skills included John Leleu who plied a successful trade with London Welsh, Swansea and Llanelli. David Pickering scored two tries at Murrayfield in 1985 to seal a Welsh victory by 25-22 and was later to achieve renown as coach Graham Henry's right-hand man. Gwyn Jones's career was tragically cut short by a neck injury just as he seemed about to fulfil the great promise he had shown from an early age.

No doubt the predatory nature of the flanker's trade will survive long into the new Millennium. All Welsh rugby supporters hope that the Valleys will produce heroes to follow in the thundering and threatening footsteps of Thomas, Morgan and Taylor, to quicken the heartbeat of adversaries large and small. No doubt the smell of a good lathering of liniment will herald an impending all-embracing tackle as another heroic Welsh flanker bears down on fearful opponents.

Rugby supporters are prone to similes when extolling the virtues of their heroes. So lineout forwards are compared to leaping salmon and the second row of forwards is often described as the scrum's boilerhouse. For players to meld both these attributes into one is nothing if not startling. Wales has provided its supporters with plenty of opportunity to reach for its store of similes when assessing the merits of its second-row forwards.

Although their memory may be fading, many old stagers wax lyrical about the 'great' Roy John of Neath, whose tall, athletic frame set the standard for second-row forwards. Later known as 'lock forwards,' as they locked their team's pack into a united and cohesive force, these giants of the rugby field send smaller opponents scattering if they have the chance to run with the ball. Often hunting in pairs, as they spend so much of the game in semi-embrace with their fellow second-row forward, greatness has come for some in tandem. Roy John was fortunate to be nurtured by an even greater hero for Neath and Wales, Rees Stephens, who played for his country on 32 occasions. The pair also made the 1950 Lions tour to the Antipodes.

R H (Rhys) Williams of Llanelli took the baton on from Stephens and John for the Lions tour of South Africa in 1955 and the memory sometimes deceives one that R H formed a formidable partnership with W R (Roddy) Evans as they toured 'Down Under' with the 1959 Lions. They only played a handful of games together, in fact, and Evans's law studies (he won a Cambridge Blue before becoming a solicitor in Bridgend) curtailed a career which might otherwise have led him to greatness. R H and W R set the standard in combining prowess in the second row and academic success. R H Williams worked as a research chemist after graduating. Hard on the heels of these two, albeit as little more than a flash-in-the-pan on the Welsh international scene, came Keith Rowlands, who played some formidable club

Robert Norster

rugby for both Llanelli and Cardiff and was a considerable force on the 1962 Lions tour of South Africa. He was later to become one of the game's leading administrators, culminating in his tenure of the post of Secretary of the International Rugby Board (the IRB).

Obstructing Rowlands in his quest for a regular place in the national team were a pair of locks whose range of skills complemented each other in the powerhouse of the Welsh scrum. They both achieved on different occasions a degree of notoriety which (although in keeping with the image of the second row as villains) still tarnishes the memory of their greatness. Brian Thomas of Neath, a Cambridge blue who became a metallurgist at the huge steelworks at Port Talbot and later a most able administrator of his home-town club, was equalled by few in his day as a tight forward. Hitting rucks with great power and ripping the ball from the opposition's grasp almost at will, this giant of a forward (compared to his contemporaries) was feared throughout the land for his great strength. Alongside him for Wales on nine occasions was a lineout jumper in the Roy John mould. Brian Price of Newport first made an impact on the big time in the Barbarians' famous victory against the touring Springboks in 1961 and became a cornerstone of Clive Rowlands's Triple Crown team of 1965, as well as captaining his country's team successfully in 1969. Price seemed, at times, to hang in the air, in those long-gone days when forwards had to jump unaided.

Sadly, though, the image that sticks in the mind is that of a shocked Brian Price, hardly believing that he had just laid out Irish flanker Noel Murphy, during the 1969 Triple Crown decider at Cardiff with an uppercut of which any boxer would have been proud. It was obvious that Price was full of remorse, this otherwise sporting player having allowed his own high standards to lapse just the once in an exemplary career. Welsh rugby and Brian Thomas's name was also tarnished in the match against England in the Triple Crown season of 1965. Wales won 14-3 but afterwards, Thomas was accused of having bitten the cheek of England centre, Geoff Frankcom, a colleague of

Thomas's in the successful Cambridge University team of the early 1960s. The Welsh Rugby Union did not pick Thomas for the remainder of the season although he won three caps the following year. Sad as these two events were, Thomas and Price are still revered in Wales as one of the best pairings to have played in the second row.

While R H Williams is still fondly remembered at Stradey Park, most West Walians hold one particular Llanelli lock in even greater esteem. Delme Thomas, from the village of Bancyfelin near Carmarthen, had earned his spurs as a raw, uncapped tourist with the 1966 Lions in Australia and New Zealand, playing in two Tests. He also played in two Tests for the Lions in South Africa in 1968 and a further two back in New Zealand in 1971. On that last trip the tourists were coached by the great Carwyn James, the mastermind who also coached Delme Thomas's club to their almost incredible victory against the All Blacks in 1972. A Welshman to the core, Thomas was a surprisingly quiet man on and off the field but as a lock forward he ruled the lineout. After his first Lions tour, he made his debut for his country against Australia in 1966, thereafter playing 25 matches for Wales. He dominated the lineout for Wales until his retirement in 1973, having left an indelible mark on club and country. Closer to home, Delme Thomas will always be remembered for that day when, although a giant, he was carried shoulder high off the field after his club's historic victory over the All Blacks.

Much has been written and spoken about Welsh rugby's last 'Golden Age' in the late 1970s, when the national team won two Grand Slams and four Triple Crowns. Invariably, the backs are seen as the catalysts who scored the points and thus won the matches. It must always be remembered that the hard-working forwards usually have to win the ball and present it to the backs to weave their magic. So it was with that great team of the 1970s, blessed with a particularly effective second row pairing in Allan Martin of Aberavon and Geoff Wheel of Swansea.

Martin was, in the mould of Roy John, Brian Price and Delme Thomas, an excellent lineout jumper and quite a competent goalkicker for his club. Allan Martin played his most effective game for his country in the Grand Slam decider against France at Cardiff in 1978. Consistently winning quality lineout ball and with scrummaging, mauling and rucking of the highest order, Martin set Wales on the path towards a great victory by 16 points to 7.

Wheel was without peer in the maul, ripping the ball from the grasp of opponents at will and creating a platform from which the backs could attack yet again. As with Brian Thomas a dozen years earlier, Wheel sailed close to the legal wind at times and regretfully he was dismissed in 1977 for foul play, along with Ireland's Willie Duggan. Martin and Wheel may have to play second fiddle in the history books, taking a back seat to the star backs of their day but they remain heroes to all who admire effective second-row play.

At the end of the 1990s there was one particular young man who hoped to be one of the great lock forwards of Welsh rugby. Ian Gough played for both Newport and Pontypridd before establishing himself in the national team, in keeping with the increasing mobility of players between clubs since the advent of the professional game. A dozen years earlier and Gough might have stayed put in his native Pontypool or at least made the one move to Newport and established himself as a cornerstone of the black-and-ambers pack.

One player who dominated lineout at home and abroad for his one club and his country was Robert Norster, who was the mainstay of the Cardiff pack in the 1980s and who was often his country's sole source of usable possession. Anyone with only a vague memory of Wales's astonishing 12-9 victory against England in Cardiff in 1989 would swear that Norster's titanic efforts had won every lineout that day against the formidable English pair of Dooley and Ackford. Norster remained a one-club man as well as being the Welsh team manager under coach Alan Davies in the early 1990s. He has subsequently put his experience to good use as the Cardiff team manager in the early years of professional rugby union.

One Welsh international lock forward who remained loyal to one club throughout his career and who might have benefited from playing in one position was Llanelli's Phil Davies. A mountain of a man at club level, able to switch at will between lock, No. 8 and blindside flanker, Davies never quite achieved international greatness, probably because he was willing to sacrifice personal glory for the benefit of his club by playing wherever club (and eventually, country) needed him. A tower of strength in adversity, Phil Davies showed his versatility by scoring Wales's only try from No. 8 in a 34-6 defeat at Twickenham in 1990 but led his club to Welsh Cup glory the following season while playing at lock. Playing alongside English-born Welsh international lock, Tony Copsey, Davies attained the heights (literally) with Llanelli. The fans who thronged to Llanelli in the early 1990s longed to see Davies and Copsey given an extended run in the national team, to see if they could transfer their club success to the higher level.

Whatever success or failure Welsh international teams achieve, lock forwards will reach the heights. Law changes may or may not allow lifting at the lineout but, come what may, these giants will invariably stand head and shoulders above the majority of their team-mates, providing the power in the scrum when required. Although dismissed by some lightweight backs almost as a necessary evil, the memory of Roy John, Brian Price, Delme Thomas and Bob Norster leaping at the lineout will earn this particular breed of rugby player a well-earned place in the pantheon of Welsh heroes.

HOOKER

Neither the word 'hooker' nor its Welsh equivalent 'bachwr' really do justice to the man who faces the opposition in the middle of the front row to dispute possession in the scrum. Nothing compares with the French '*talonneur*' to describe this player's specialist role scraping the ball back into his team's half of the scrum. Many Welsh rugby supporters, though, when asked about '*talons*' in the context of a hooker, will only remember the gruesome photograph of Garin Jenkins taken during the 1999 World Cup, his eyes seemingly being gouged by an Argentinean opponent. Jenkins has, by now, become the most capped Welsh international hooker and, despite not being a member of a successful national team, he has earned himself a reputation as a fiery and uncompromising hero on the rugby field.

The words 'fiery' and 'uncompromising' are almost prerequisites for describing hookers. Standing there, waiting for the scrum to form, each arm around the shoulders of their props, they are a particularly vulnerable breed of rugby player. In the modern game, not only do they need to be mobile and brave but also to be able to throw the ball with unerring accuracy to their lineout jumpers. While Garin Jenkins has reigned supreme in the role for much of the 1990s, his position has been under constant threat from Robin McBryde, Jonathan Humphreys and Barrie Williams, each of whom brought different skills to their game. Williams did not always catch the eye of the Welsh selectors but he won a place on the Lions tour of South Africa in 1997. Many of his supporters in Neath and Llandovery expected Williams to make the position his own for a number of years. Sadly it was not to be and it has been left to the others to contest the position. Humphreys captained his country in the mid-1990s at a time when achievement rarely matched expectation.

Another many hoped would be part of a successful Welsh team was Kevin

Phillips of Neath. Fortunate enough to be propped by able internationals Jeremy Pugh and Brian Williams and later John Davies (who, like Phillips and Williams, was a North Pembrokeshire farmer), Kevin Phillips was a human dynamo on the field. Anyone who witnessed his all-action leadership of his Neath club against the 1989 New Zealand All Blacks could only have been inspired by the man. One spectator, indeed, ran onto the field at the end intending to tackle English referee, Fred Howard, and had to be restrained by Bedford touch-judge, Ian Bullerwell!

Sadly, Phillips did not achieve greatness in the red of Wales and was never really in contention for a Lions tour. The same fate befell Norman Gale of Llanelli, a larger-than-life character who hooked for Swansea before becoming a cult figure in the scarlet of Llanelli and Wales in the mid-1960s. Eventually destined to captain his country against Brian Lochore's touring All Blacks in 1967, Gale was an abrasive player who gave the opposition no quarter. At the end of his career he was only marginally slower than young Scarlets outside-half, Phil Bennett, in 100-yard sprints during club training sessions. An integral part of Clive Rowlands's Triple Crown-winning team in 1965, Norman Gale was not averse to taking over goalkicking duties for club and country if necessary – with surprising success.

In spite of his domestic and international success, Norman Gale suffers by comparison with his immediate predecessor. Bryn Meredith of Newport first played for Wales in 1954 as a raw student at St Luke's College, Exeter, and a little over a year later was an integral part of the Lions pack in South Africa, when a great team managed to share a four-Test series with the Springboks. Playing 34 times for his country, Meredith was, for a number of years, Wales's most-capped forward. Despite being ousted as first-choice hooker on the Lions tour to the Antipodes in 1959 by tour captain, Ronnie Dawson of Ireland, Bryn Meredith returned to South Africa with Arthur Smith's 1962 Lions. Despite (in rugby-playing terms) advancing years, he had retained his mobility and, in tandem with the great Irish prop Syd Millar, performed magnificently in both tight and loose play. Like many supporters at home, he was saddened by the defensive and inhibited rugby played by the tourists. This was not the end that Bryn Meredith's career deserved.

Another hooker who achieved heroic status during a highly successful playing career acquired the title of 'Duke' among his playing peers. Bobby Windsor, the central figure of the famed Pontypool front row of the 1970s, did not have his title bestowed upon his powerful shoulders by royalty but by jocular friend and foe as he bestrode the rugby field for his club, his country and the British Lions. An integral part of the Lions pack during the successful tour of South Africa in 1974, 'Duke' Windsor brought a down-to-earth valleys humour to scrums throughout the rugby-playing world. His consistency in striking for scrum ball, coupled with dynamic loose play and accurate throwing into the lineout secured him a place in the successful Welsh team of the late 1970s. When his international playing days were over Windsor was still keen enough to turn out for his beloved Pontypool. Having borne the tragedy of losing his young wife and having to raise his children as a single parent, a frightening back injury against Bedford at Goldington Road seemed to condemn him to a life at best confined to a wheelchair. Such was his determination, however, that he made a surprisingly rapid recovery.

The hooker can achieve fame and, in the professional age, fortune despite being buried in the nether regions of the scrum. Jeff Young of London Welsh, who hooked for the 1971 Grand Slam team and toured with the 1968 Lions, was later to become a very able technical officer for the WRU, imparting his vast knowledge of the game to later generations of players. D M Davies was an uncompromising Somerset policeman who played an integral role as hooker in Wales's Grand Slams of 1950 and 1952. Like Young, he was a Lion, this time in 1950, but had to play second fiddle to the Irishman who led the party – tour captain, fellow hooker and master tactician, Karl Mullen.

It may, at times, be difficult to think of hookers (who spend so much of their time in the darkest recesses of the scrum) as stars of the rugby field. Rare

Bobby Windsor

are the days when hookers are as recognised as the 'Fancy Dans' of the threequarter line. They give no quarter however, when facing menacing opponents in the heat of scrum and maul. Spectators may be grudging in their admiration but members of the front-row fraternity know that the likes of Bryn Meredith, Bobby Windsor and Garin Jenkins have been the prime source of set-piece possession for the glamorous runners in the wide-open spaces.

"Can you imagine what it would be like to be working two miles underground at the coal face one minute then have to run as fast as you could the next, carrying all your tools, back up to ground level and a mile down the valley for a quick stint at the blast furnace in the local ironworks before retracing your steps to fill the next wagon of coal."

Thus was the life of a rugby union prop forward described to me when, as a somewhat green young referee, I was confronted in the bar after a particularly bruising encounter by the four rock-hard gentlemen who had spent the afternoon knocking lumps out of each other, now engaged in full-on, arms-around-each-other's-shoulders, just-short-of-kissing bonhomie! Prop forwards are a different breed. Sometimes a cross between a weightlifter and a sumo wrestler, they always look mean but often have a touch of the cuddly teddy bear to keep the female rugby supporter interested.

The sight, therefore, of a prop forward cantering 70 metres, ball in hand, bedraggled would-be tacklers trailing forlornly behind, to score as spectacular a try as any scampering threequarter is not a frequent occurrence. Graham Price, a member of the famous Pontypool and Wales front row of the late 1970s, nicknamed by some as 'The Viet Gwent' in an allusion to the former South-East Asian guerillas, had everyone cheering to the rafters as he did exactly that, scoring (on his international debut in 1975) one of Wales's five tries in their only victory at the Parc des Princes. Little did we know, on that famous day in Paris, that Price was to be the cornerstone of the Welsh pack for the next decade, involved in two Grand Slams and four Triple Crowns and touring with three Lions teams (1977, 1980 and 1983). Although some wag on that cold January afternoon across the Channel did suggest that the stadium should be re-christened the 'Parc de Price'!

It is perhaps more difficult to assess from the grandstand the real worth to a team of a prop than almost any other position. Not for him the glamour of the sidestep (other than of the 'Maori' ilk), the swerve, nor even the glory of claiming the strike against the head at the scrum although few hookers would deny the assistance given to them by efficient scrummagers. Wales has a fine lineage of accomplished scrummaging prop forwards, culminating in the 1990s with a number of players vying for a regular place in the national team. Durability was the hallmark of David Young, captain of the Welsh team at the end of the Millennium, having made his international bow during the inaugural World Cup tournament in 1987. Alongside him Darren Morris, Spencer John, Chris Anthony and others compete for a toehold on greatness much as they fight to plant their feet solidly in the turf as they anchor the scrum.

Graham Price was most fortunate in playing his early international matches as part of a settled club front row. With hooker Bobby Windsor and fellow-prop, Charlie Faulkner, alongside him, Price did not need to spend pre-match days getting to know his colleagues at the coalface. He all but slept with them already. No Welsh front-row unit has managed to get anywhere near the Pontypool trio in terms of collective ability and achievement. Wales has, however, produced other cohesive units, most notably in the mid-1950s when Courteney Meredith of Neath teamed up with W O ('Billy') Williams of Swansea to prop hooker Bryn Meredith of Newport. They may have been from three different clubs but they formed a front row both exciting and solid. It was effective enough to earn all three players places on the Lions tour of South Africa in 1955. The props so nursed Bryn Meredith through his early international career (not that he needed much nursing) that he remained at the top from 1954 to the Lions tour to South Africa in 1962. Billy Williams, famed for his homesickness for West Wales whenever he was away with Wales or the Lions, was versatile enough to switch from his international position to play just as effectively in the second row for his club.

Homesickness is a strange trait to find in a prop forward, especially with

Graham Price

the image of hardness inherent in the breed's make-up. It is, therefore, surprising to hear that another great Welsh propping hero, Ray Prosser, felt the same emotional tug for his native land when on tour in Australia, New Zealand and Canada with the 1959 Lions. Prosser won 22 Welsh caps from 1956 to 1961 but the fame he attained during his playing days was outstripped by his achievement as the coach of the all-conquering Pontypool in the 1970s and 1980s. In the modern set-up, with specialist coaches assigned to each component part of a team, a younger Ray Prosser might well have been called upon to impart his profound knowledge of front-row play and of scrummaging technique to the current crop of players. It is doubtful whether he would have been any happier, however, than when he played for and then coached his beloved 'Pooler'.

The craggy features of some battle-hardened props seem, at times, to have been hewn from the coalface where many of their ancestors toiled. Some props laboured hard there themselves even on a morning of the match. Many fans still have vivid memories of a valley train being held up on the way to an international match in Cardiff to let a player (more often than not a prop) climb on board for the kick-off a couple of hours later. I have a vague recollection of a prop getting on the Fishguard to London Express on the morning of an international, settling down for a snooze in the corner of the compartment after an urgent plea, "Don't let me sleep past Cardiff, boys. Don't want to let the side down now, do we?" One of my fellow travellers, obviously in the know and not so open-mouthed awe-struck as I was, announced that, "That man has just hewn a couple of tons of anthracite while you boys were in the land of nod. Now he's going to show those white-shirted so-and-sos what for, down a few pints of dark and then dig some more coal while you're all cwtshed up tonight." My mouth fell open another couple of inches as I realised that this really hard man was sleeping like a baby a few feet away!

The hardness associated with the rugby prop forward has proved useful for different aspects of play. Scrummaging strength is a prerequisite for the position together with the ability to take immense pressure against one or both shoulders when playing on either the loose- or tight-head of the scrum. The ability to rip the ball from the grasp of an opponent is also an indication of a prop's strength. No-one matched Brian Williams in this area of play in the early 1990s as he formed the cornerstone of an all-Preseli front row at Neath with hooker Kevin Phillips and fellow-prop John Davies, who was young enough to continue playing into the professional era with Richmond and Llanelli. Sadly for all three, they played their international rugby in an era when their country struggled just to keep up with developments elsewhere.

Other props aimed for but failed to attain immortality for their exploits. Cliff Davies and J D Robins both went on the 1950 Lions tour of New Zealand, Australia and Ceylon (a curious place to play rugby in those far-off days) but, as part of an inherently lightweight Lions pack, failed to set their exciting backs free to dominate. Robins enhanced his reputation as Assistant Manager and Coach of the 1966 Lions in New Zealand although a torn achilles tendon curtailed his activities on the training field. A number of commentators assert that Robins, following the Irish hooker who captained the 1959 Lions, Ronnie Dawson, prepared the ground for Carwyn James's success in 1971 by advocating that one member of the tourists' management team should, in future, be a coach. How far from present day teams of specialist coaches for each and every aspect of play.

In that 1966 Lions party was another international prop who occasionally played for Ebbw Vale in the second row. Denzil Williams's international career spanned the years 1963-71 and he and John Dawes were the only playing link between Clive Rowlands's Triple Crown team of 1965 and Dawes's Grand Slam winners in 1971. In that latter team, Williams shared propping duties with Bridgend star John Lloyd, a technically brilliant and exceptionally fit player whose physique let him down somewhat at the highest level. In another era, Lloyd might have been a Lions selection and achieved the truly heroic status which just eluded him, a player who always put his body on the line for his country, whatever the playing conditions.

Another star who shone briefly for Wales and for the Lions was K D (Kingsley) Jones, not to be confused with his later namesake, the flanker from Ebbw Vale and Gloucester. 'K D' won only 10 caps for his country in the early 1960s and toured South Africa with the 1962 Lions but friend and foe had nothing but fear and dread for his scrummaging ability. This talent resurfaced in the Welsh front row in 1999 in Peter Rogers, like K D Jones a former pupil of one of the great nurseries of Welsh rugby players, Llandovery College in Carmarthenshire.

As a referee, one lived in constant dread of the props' perennial admonishment, "You couldn't possibly have seen that, Ref!" Prop forwards are a law unto themselves at times but always great characters. Heroes all, too, for braving the coalface and the blast furnace of the rugby scrum. Ask the average rugby fan to expand on the technicalities of propping, and their eyes immediately glaze over. Far better to pay our respects, show our admiration and hope that, somewhere over the horizon, there is a clone of Graham Price ready, able and waiting to do the business for Wales.

Post Script

Despite my earlier promise not to enter those choppiest of Welsh rugby waters by naming a 'Greatest' team, I have been urged to create an almighty ruck by listing a team that, had they played together, I would have liked to watch. It is a team which, with a little bit of help from the elements and the bounce of the ball, would have given any opponents a cracking good game and, to my view, a good beating! Why not compare my team with yours?

15. J P R Williams

14. Gerald Davies

13. Bleddyn Williams

12. Steve Fenwick

11. J J Williams

10. Phil Bennett (no relation!)

9. Gareth Edwards

1. Courtney Meredith

2. Bryn Meredith

3. Graham Price

4. R H Williams

5. Rees Stephens

6. Derek Quinnell

7. Haydn Morgan

8. Mervyn Davies

***

Shortly before publication, I discussed the manuscript with a friend who is an out-and-out Cardiff supporter, despite the fact that his roots are firmly in the soil of a Gwent valley. His first comment was, "What about Rex Willis? You can't leave Willis out! He may have only been a Cardiff, Wales and Lions scrum half, but he never played for Llanelli! And what about Jeff Squire? A star No. 8 for Pontypool, Wales and the Lions, and he doesn't get a mention! How can you leave out Eddie Butler, another Pontypool and Wales No. 8, now transformed into a star pundit on television? Yes, I know he spent most of his playing days with his head wedged between two colleagues' backsides, but you've got to mention *him* or the book will be slated! And what about so-and-so…? And what about…?"

The stuff of nightmares indeed. I know only too well that I have omitted too many heroes and the occasional villain, such as… No, I'd better not mention them, just in case the libel lawyers are sharpening their quills and getting their briefs in a twist.

All I can add is that, if you find that your particular hero is not mentioned between these covers, just ask yourself, "Was he *that* good?" Or perhaps there are far more Welsh Rugby Heroes than any one supporter is willing to acknowledge!

– Wales within your reach:
an attractive series
at attractive prices!

Titles already published:

1. Welsh Talk
Heini Gruffudd
086243 447 5
£2.95

2. Welsh Dishes
Rhian Williams
086243 492 0
£2.95

3. Welsh Songs
Lefi Gruffudd (ed.)
086243 525 0
£3.95

4. Welsh Mountain Walks
Dafydd Andrews
086243 547 1
£3.95

5. Welsh Organic Recipes
Dave and Barbara Frost
086243 574 9
£3.95

6. Welsh Railways
Jim Green
086243 551 X
£3.95

7. Welsh Place Names
Brian Davies
086243 514 5
£3.95

8. Welsh Castles
Geraint Roberts
086243 550 1
£3.95

9. Welsh Rugby Heroes
Androw Bennett
086243 552 8
£3.95

Also to be published in the *It's Wales* series:

Welsh National Heroes

Welsh Games for Children

Welsh Jokes